D1249525

My Silent Story
The Gun That Saved My Life

Jordon Johnson Chisti

My Silent Story

Copyright © 2022 Jordon Johnson Chisti

My Silent Story-The Gun That Saved My Life
By Jordon Johnson Chisti

Printed in the United States of America

ISBN 979-8-9857315-2-1

www.paprovipublishing.com

Pa-Pro-Vi
PUBLISHING

TABLE OF CONTENTS

ACKNOWLEDGMENTS

Pausing for a moment...

Throughout my life, I have learned to slow down and take a moment to appreciate moments, gifts, that are arising. As you are about to embark on reading this book, I take a moment to pause and express my gratitude for a few people who supported, guided, and lifted up my spirits along the way.

Thank you Jim, Daddy Wags Editing, for sharing your insight about ways to write a book and continued guidance to make me consider the language I am using and structure of this memoir. Thank you Ashley Bomgaars, for capturing the vibrancy of the messenger on the cover and the beauty of the elements through your lens.

To my lifelong love Kristy Marie, I am deeply blessed for you being who you are and by my side as this book launches into the world. I am tremendously grateful for all your love and support as we walk our path together, share the beauty of life and all it has to offer us. And, a special appreciation for our family.

My Silent Story

CHAPTER 1
NO ONE HEARD

At 2:15 p.m. on April 6, 1989, the alarm on my stopwatch went off.

My emotions were numb as I lifted the gun to my chest, pointed it at my heart, and pulled the trigger. Finally, I had made the decision that I was done with living in this world.

After months of planning, the day had finally arrived for peace to enter my life, peace to enter my heart. I was tired of hurting and wondering what I had done to deserve the life circumstances I had faced. I was done living in pain. I saw my relatives at a family gathering a few months prior and my mom again one last time over the Easter holiday weekend.

I planned my funeral, wrote it out and left it on the bed, so no one would have to worry about pulling it together. I decided to kill myself on a Thursday so people would have Friday off if needed and go back to their lives on Monday. The funeral would be early the following week.

The sound of the gun blast rippled through the school chapel as I sat in the pew waiting for someone, anyone, to rush through the door. Certainly, I thought, someone had to wonder what made that loud and explosive sound. As I looked over at the side door of the chapel, no one came rushing through the door.

But wait, why was I still conscious? Did the gun work? This was not part of the plan.

I looked down at my chest to see a small black hole in my shirt and sat there wondering what had happened. Never did I imagine being conscious after pulling the trigger.

I looked at the gun and let it drop on the floor in the aisle next to the pew. I contemplated what to do next.

No one was rushing through the side door to see what had happened even though the senior lounge was adjacent to the chapel.

I gently rested my head on the pew in front of me, hoping that sooner than later I would fall asleep, I would die. Eventually, I lay down in the pew and tried to hold my breath. If I held it long enough, I would pass out. I would die.

Every time I tried to hold my breath, I would gasp for air. My eyes closed, blood filling my lungs and slowly trickling onto the pew where I lay.

That day changed my life in more ways than one.

For years, I had contemplated ending my life. Ever since I was about 9 years old, I struggled with suicidal thoughts. I had explored all of the options of ending my life that seemed possible. Drowning. Jumping off a cliff. Lighting myself on fire and burning up into ashes. For some reason, I never considered slashing my wrists or overdosing on pills.

I would swim at the pool in the apartment complex we were living at and try holding my breath underwater. I would give up and come up for air. I'd walk to the edge of a cliff and stand there looking over, sitting down wondering what would happen if I jumped. Would I just break my legs or lay there alive until someone found me?

I ran by the cliff that I considered jumping off the other day and all my feelings and thoughts came rushing back. Reflected on my thought process immediately, would my legs break or would I successfully kill myself if I jumped.

I was tired of living with intense emotional pain. I had given up on having any faith that my life would be different. Death would be the only solution,

I reasoned, to find peace in my heart. Never again would I have to worry about how I could survive, in peace, in this world.

I was 17 years old, terrified of graduating from high school, unsure of where I wanted life to take me, scared about financially supporting myself, and realizing that the only time I truly felt confident, about anything, was when I was playing basketball.

As a kid, I struggled. No stability in my home life. Mom struggled to find jobs that would bring financial security to her life and mine. I was tired and wanted relief. I was done with life.

Today, recalling the moment I pulled the trigger, it was like it happened 5 minutes ago. I still hear the sound of the gun going off, sitting waiting to die and the voices murmuring when I was found. Voices were faint as I was rolled out to the ambulance and the EMT's were talking on the way to the emergency room. Vaguely I captured a few words being spoken about my status at the hospital.

People were swarmed around me and before you know it my arms were stretched out to my side in the emergency room. Here we go! A sharp pain went racing through my left side and I screamed. I remember breaking away from the nurses or doctors who were holding my arms out while they cut me open to insert a chest tube to drain blood from my lungs. I was screaming at the doctor inserting the tube. No anesthesia given. No time to waste. My body was in shock. Suddenly, voices were telling me that other tubes also would be put into my body. I felt a tube go slithering down my nose.

I can see the doctors and nurses and interns standing at the foot of my hospital bed as I lifted my head. Get a blanket, I begged, I'm cold. Their faces were almost a blank slate. Who was more in shock? Them? Or me? I didn't know. I'm cold, I'm cold, I kept telling them. I was dying. That's why I was cold and shivering. The clock was ticking as time was running out to save me.

As I was rolled out to have surgery, I heard a woman crying hysterically in the hallway. Was that my aunt? What was happening? I had no idea of what I looked like as I thought I was dying.

That was the first day of the rest of my life, at age 17. Little did I realize how my life was about to change.

CHAPTER 2
UNFOLDING OF LIFE

My life continues to unfold. It always will change. I am in a space of job transition, and I am trying to navigate the working world in which we are expected to engage. I am struggling to accept my self-worth and lean into my beliefs that a career position is coming. Daily, I lean on my faith and trust the universe's process of ensuring my life does not stray from the path meant for me. This is one of the reasons I wrote this book and shared my experiences of facing hopelessness, walking through fear, and making decisions to move forward in my life, even if it means being alone. I am an only child so I know what it means to feel alone and be by myself. The beauty is I am never alone.

When I was laying in the hospital bed about a week after my suicide attempt, I said to myself that no one should ever have to feel as hopeless as I felt and that the only solution to find peace was to end one's life. I thought killing myself was the sole answer to finding peace in my heart. All I wanted was to have peace in my heart.

I do remember a moment in the emergency room, dying, and I turned my head to one of the nurses or doctors and clearly stated that I did not want to die.

Over the course of my life, a sense of hopelessness has emerged over and over. As an adolescent, I did not fully understand the depth of my hopelessness. But with the passage of time, I have learned to utilize personal tools to shift my thinking about different situations, whether they were jobs, finances, relationships, school, or self-confidence. The intense fear that overcomes people like me, trying to cope and manage and fit in and survive can make day-to-day life a huge challenge. Trying to navigate the expectations society puts on you can be a huge burden. I have lived with enormous tension, from a constant state of survival mode as a result of being raised in extreme poverty to managing my own financial responsibilities to pay the rent, make the car payment, keep up to date on insurance premiums and credit card bills. Finances are a stressor in my life that exhausts me and I have learned how to navigate those stressors.

I have struggled with accepting where I am

financially and not trying to get roped into a materialistic life where I live beyond my means. Finally, I have found some peace in how to manage my finances. But there was a day when I had no one to help me figure out how to manage money. My aunt probably was the best teacher: She advised me to save $5 of every paycheck and to stash it away somewhere. Eventually, those $5 bills would add up to a handsome sum, she said. Saving five dollars has come in handy when money gets tight until my next paycheck. I have put gas in my car to get to work for the week. I have bought a few groceries to tide me over. I have also saved enough money to take a trip without having to go into debt.

And to this day, I practice that habit to the best of my ability.

I realized years ago that I did not want to struggle my entire life financially or feel like I was trying to survive day by day all over again. At one time, I was a victim of credit-card debt, trying to keep up materialistically with friends and family and it seemed like everyone else. For a while, I had created the illusion of financial comfort by the things I bought and collected—when in reality, I was constantly struggling to make it to the next paycheck. Living within my means was a foreign concept.

My mother always presented the public face that we were financially secure and living a high quality life when in reality we were struggling to put a meal on the table that was better than candy bars and donuts. We had an apartment, but we also had eviction notices on our door.

I have dug myself out of debt in the past only to find myself back in it again because of my insecurities.

Today, I can finally say with some confidence that I have escaped from this pattern of living an illusionary life, especially based in finances.

I thought money would provide some sense of happiness. Once, I thought buying a motorcycle would bring me joy and fulfillment in my life. I took classes to learn to drive and get my license. Yet, the motorcycle did not resolve the struggles internally with figuring out who I was and what I wanted to do in my life.

I was generous with my money only to be taken advantage at different points in my life. I had friends assume that I would pay for their portion of a bill when eating out. The bill often would include expensive alcoholic drinks along with their meals. Finally, I decided that I was tired of feeling used financially by people. It was a tough lesson that I had to learn, yet I am more than willing to be generous in my life, if possible. For instance, I do not mind paying for a meal or movie at times. When I have limited funds, I am still willing to contribute or offer to pay for things. Holding on tightly to money is not useful to me. Being thoughtful about the funds I have available is different than clenching my fists around every dollar in my pocket.

For myself, I have come to learn that money will always show up when needed if I keep myself open to a give and receiving process. I need to have that constant flow of money moving in my life along with being thoughtful about how I spend and save my dollars. It is a practice that I am still engaged with every day.

I also decided to surround myself with people who did not take advantage of my generosity or willingness to reach into my wallet to pay for things. I accepted responsibility for the debt I accumulated, even though a few people suggested that I file bankruptcy. Because I was insecure, unable to stand up for my values, and allowed people to take advantage of me, I felt responsible for my financial situation. I sought financial guidance on how to consolidate debt in order to pay it off in a timely manner. I realize money management is about being disciplined and clear with my self about the reality of my financial situation. This is a lesson that I did not learn growing up. I learned to keep an image about a certain financial status that was not true.

Over the years, I have learned not to be ashamed of my circumstances, even though it is a daily practice, yet to forgive myself for getting lost in a cultural narrative about what I should and should not have, which does not align with my way of being.

Life is tricky. Often, I live one day at a time, knowing the universe has my best interest in its hands. I trust this process and leaning into the flow of my life. The flow of money manifests in my life through giving and receiving.

When I was 17 years old, and even at points later in my life, I knew I did not want to die. Yet I did not fully understand how to live in this society/world. I did not understand what it meant to be true to and believe deeply in who you are as a person. I decided to be who I am and let go of the cultural expectations and narratives that circulate constantly about how one is supposed to live their life.

I have come to appreciate that life is constantly unfolding before my eyes. I need to listen to the messengers, walk through fear when needed, and show up daily. The small (and big) gifts will present themselves when I let go of trying to always control the outcomes.

This book, these chapters, my story, is about reaching out to others who feel a sense of hopelessness or are lost and are just trying to make it through the day. The book is about not being silenced, about struggling in this society, navigating a culture of chaos and anxiety, and being present for life's circumstances as they emerge. The question should be, "Who am I not to share my story?" I am not invested in the silence that keeps me disconnected from other people. An abundance of hopefulness exists in this world, priceless connections, yet these feelings are a challenge to document and measure.

Facing hopelessness, processing self-doubt, and developing a practice of listening to one's surroundings are described on the following pages.

I sat in the hospital bed reflecting on the fact that I faced my life ending by my own hand, which resulted in major surgeries, losing a portion of a lung, and scars to remember every moment. I was unaware of the lifetime commitment and daily practices necessary to reflect on my life, my values, my beliefs, and my path, way of being in walking through this world especially leading me to pull the trigger of the gun pointed at my heart.

None of this is to say that life has been a bowl of cherries, that I have the tiger by the tail. There have been stretches of hopelessness, reminders of that low moment with a gun in my hand. Yet I am still alive. Fear, anger, sadness, joy, and a multitude of other emotions course through my blood and skin, telling me I'm alive. I did not die in any way––physically, emotionally, spiritually––even though I had no idea how to live in this society/world, given the cultural expectations and narratives constantly coming at me about who I was supposed to be.

Now, instead of getting hooked into other people's fears, anxieties, expectations, or directions in life, I pay close attention to what makes the most sense for me.

CHAPTER 3

THE BITTER COLD

The bitter cold air breezes through my coat as I walk down the street on a Minnesota winter night to sleep at a hotel. I'm chilled to the bones, scarf wrapped around my face, eyes barely open due to exhaustion and being frosted over. No guarantee on a room waiting for us when we arrive. The comfort of a hotel bed, blankets, and watching television is in question.

When hotel rooms still had keys to open the doors, Mom would keep the key from a previous night, and sometimes we would sneak into a room to stay for the night. We would sleep on top of the covers, had to be extremely quiet, and we would depart, nearly silently, early in the morning. No trace that we had ever been in the room. It was a clever way to have a warm place to stay because there was no money to spare for a room or even a meal.

Living day-to-day and unsure what the next day might bring became familiar. I cannot recall how many places we stayed or moved throughout my adolescence.

When I was about 14, we moved to Minneapolis, which was supposed to bring financial relief and stability in our lives. I was hoping for an apartment to call home for a while where we would have meals around a table. My mom would work a steady job, and she did work. She worked multiple jobs and crazy hours at times. She worked at a restaurant to assist them with their bookkeeping, I think, and began at 4:00 am or something like that. I remember waiting at the mall for her to be done with working at Dayton's, now Macy's, before we would head out to find a place to stay for the night.

Yet the following year, I was ready to move back to Duluth. The big city just wasn't for me. I went from a school with a class of 44 people to having over hundreds of classmates. I felt lost and could not figure out how to connect with people. I was tired of eviction notices, secret phone ring codes, having to hide in our home if someone came knocking on the door, and sleeping in random places when needed.

I was raised in Duluth, a beautiful city in northern Minnesota. It is on Lake Superior, where I spent times as a young child skipping rocks, enjoying the sunshine, playing on the beach down at Park

Point, and learning to appreciate the vastness of the lake. Being by the water became a place of calmness and reflection later in life.

Duluth was also a place I learned how to survive. Living with no money and without a consistent home.

We often stayed with friends or relatives throughout my childhood only for that to come to an end at some point. I remember tip toeing around so I did not make a mess. We basically went to the room where we slept and left early in the morning in order not to get in the way. At times, we would stay with my grandparents who lived an hour out of town.

Staying with my grandparents was comforting. My grandpa would have a dish of vanilla ice cream with chocolate sauce every night. It was a delicious treat. They would buy the 5-gallon bucket of ice cream from Schwann's. For many years, I would indulge in this tradition since it brought me a sense of peace.

We rented a house a few years during the winter months, which was the closest I felt to having a stable home in the winter. It was completely furnished. Most of our apartments we lived in were empty. My bed consisted of a blanket or two on the floor. We did not have a couch, dining room table, or any of the other household furniture pieces found in a home. At times, we had a small television where I would watch shows while eating some food. I learned to use a pillow for my table while sitting on the floor. Macaroni or noodles with butter and sugar became a stable meal. Once in a while, we had cheese to add to the noodles.

I remember staying at the Y where rooms were available to rent. It had a bed to sleep in, but we shared the living room, kitchen, and bathroom with other tenants on the floor. I remember an elderly woman who also stayed there and she would take me under her wing, from time to time. She would take me out for Sammy's pizza down the street on Fridays. It was a delicious treat. Sammy's pizza has the best thin crust sausage pizza and was one of the most popular places to eat.

Many times we stayed in the car overnight parked at the university. A blanket pulled up to my chin, the seat slightly reclined, and the engine running at times throughout the night to break the chill. Unsure what happened when we no longer had a car to sleep in as well as transport us from place to place.

Riding the bus or walking became our mode of transportation. Surviving the winter months with no real place to call home in Minnesota has ingrained in me the sacredness of having a home. The sacredness of knowing I have a roof over my head and a door to walk through to take my shoes off. I have rented the majority of my life and learned the importance of paying my rent on time. No compromise with paying rent. I compromise on buying food, clothes and going out to movies. No hesitation with paying the bill where I open the door to rest my head for the night.

A place to call home. A place to rest from the daily struggles in life. A place to feel joy and be who I am without the pressure of what other people are thinking about me. A place to call home is a place of sacredness for me.

CHAPTER 4
LOOKING IN THE MIRROR

Day after day, I would look into the mirror, imagining what it would be like to shoot myself in the head, a bullet passing through my mouth or into my heart. I would picture my funeral, my body displayed in an open casket.

When my grandparents passed away, I went to their visitations and funerals. I remember how peaceful my grandmother looked in her casket. It was important to me that I also appeared to be at peace, one last time, in my casket. If I shot myself in the head, I could not visualize how I would have an open casket at my funeral.

I would sit at the end of the bed, lifted the gun to my head, put it in my mouth, and imagined pulling the trigger. I decided over the course of time that shooting myself in the head was not an option.

Besides, my heart is what hurt. My heart carried the pain I was feeling day in and day out. My heart felt the disappointment from the years of wondering what I did wrong to deserve the life I was experiencing. The pain was intense, yet numb at the same time. I was lonely, yet did not know any differently. I was filled with rage from having to live on the streets, in secret, constantly moving from place to place. I was 17 years old and had no words to articulate what I was thinking or feeling. No one taught me to be vulnerable. Society doesn't teach us this asset. I was bombarded with shame, not feeling like I was enough and angry at the world for my life.

I would look in the mirror and imagine the peace that I hoped would come to my life. No one explained to me that you find peace in your life without having to die. Deep down in my heart, I did not really want to die. But I did not know how to live and navigate society. I needed help figuring out how to embrace who I was as an individual.

I did not know how to live with pain, rage, disappointment, and the plethora of other emotions that I was experiencing at that time and that I had experienced for years and years. All I had ever witnessed was people covering up their feelings and situations, again and again and again. All I was told was to not trust anyone and to never share anything about my life, with anyone. I could not talk about this with anyone who lived nearby. I could not give out our phone number, if we even had a phone. I could not bring friends over, because we often stayed at someone else's house, in a motel room or lived on the streets.

Trust no one. Keep my life a secret. Those were my marching orders.

Silence was my survival mode.

I was 17 and could not foresee my life ever changing. I was terrified of what that meant for me. All I could envision was not having a home and reliving what I knew growing up. We had lived in a motel room for weeks at times, eating donuts for breakfast and maybe once a week we ordered a pizza from Domino's. That day was a treat. I would lay on the bed, in the dark, and watch television shows all day long. I saw none of the possibilities life had to offer. And remember, I was just a young person in high school.

I looked in the mirror everyday. When I sat with the gun in my hand and made the decision to search for peace in death, I didn't realize I was grasping for a sliver of some sort of control. I was grasping for a sense of relief.

For months, I practiced pulling the trigger. Would I use a handgun or a shotgun? Would that make any difference? Then one I day, I decided to go with a handgun.

Was I scared of all of this? Absolutely. I didn't really want to die. Yet from where I sat, I just didn't have options.

How can we crack open the possibilities that life offers when feelings of hopelessness become overbearing? We must begin talking and teaching people about how to navigate a culture of anxiety that intensifies a person's pain and trauma from their lived experiences. Navigating and thriving in society/world is possible.

Today, years later, as I write these words, I can say that I have learned to find space for myself to feel all of my emotions—fear, anger, joy, love. I have figured out how to thrive and trust in the possibilities life has to offer even when struggles arise.

CHAPTER 5

A SENSE OF CONTROL

As an only child, I spent a great deal of time by myself. I entertained myself constantly—sometimes playing games on my own, going to the playground across the street from where we were staying, or practicing basketball to become a future Olympic athlete. I wanted to be the best basketball player that I could be and dreamed of playing professionally. However, I knew deep down that playing professional basketball was out of the question. Yet I still practiced as much as possible. I worked intensely on my jumping ability so I could slam-dunk someday. That never happened.

Playing or practicing basketball by myself was one part of my life that I enjoyed. I knew how to do it well. Dribbling between my legs, behind my back, and quickly moving the ball from one hand to the other to avoid a steal by a defender. On the basketball court, shooting hoops and doing drills on my own was where I gained confidence unconsciously. With basketball, I felt some sense of control. I could do it on my own. I worked to get better and better at making longer and longer shots and consistently hitting my free throws. The game taught me what it meant to be disciplined, to connect with other people, to work as a team, and to aim for a goal. I learned how to hear criticism and be pushed by my coaches to be one of the best players. Believe in yourself, and you'll succeed: That was the message I carry with me today, thanks to my high school coach.

Playing sports and being physically active gave me space emotionally to dream. Dream about being successful in life.

In high school, I turned away recruiters who were trying to get me to play college basketball. At the time, paying $100 to a recruiter who promised to assist me with going to college was a lot of money. I potentially could have had a full scholarship for my schooling, yet I said no. All I could think about was the amount of money it cost to hire the recruiter. I could not afford college tuition. We had no money. I was living with my aunt and uncle, and pursuing a college degree was not an option in my mind. I remember sharing with a recruiter that I was unsure if I even wanted to go to college. I did not allow myself to imagine this possibility. Why would I set myself up for disappointment?

I had already faced enough disappointment in my life. I was done exposing myself to those feelings.

During the winter of my high school senior year, my basketball coach pulled me into his office toward the end of the season. He talked to me about going to college and playing basketball. Believe in yourself is what he communicated to me. Believe in yourself, and you'll succeed.

After that conversation, I decided to apply to one of the local colleges, a small private school in town. Large universities terrified me. I was accepted into the college, yet I was placed on academic probation. My grades were not the best in high school until the last few months of my senior year. I struggled with the news of being told the school was placing me on academic probation because that also meant I couldn't play basketball during my freshman year. I was crushed.

Yet I decided to continue with school. I moved into a dorm, had a great roommate, and began learning how to live on my own. I worked throughout college at various jobs. Since I was unable to play basketball, I started running. One of my previous teammates asked if I would run a marathon the following summer. I did not hesitate to say yes and start training.

After a short while of attending classes, I realized I wanted to get out of my hometown. I didn't want to get stuck living in town for the rest of my life and have it become the only thing that I ever knew.

Taking a leap in life, I applied to a small college in Iowa and was accepted. I transferred after my first year and explored what it meant to live in a small college town in the middle of Iowa. For me, this was a huge leap and living on the edge. I moved out of state, did not know anyone, and took a chance on trying to play basketball there. I lived a life of being on the move, yet I felt secure taking this leap of living on my own.

Throughout my time in Iowa, I gained a sense of my personal struggles, and I was willing to look seriously at what I really wanted in my life. My grades still were not where they should have been, and it was a struggle, academically; I was pursuing a degree in sports administration. Sports and being physically active is what I knew how to do well. I held on to this aspect of my life unconsciously as a security mechanism. Being active and physically challenging my body also meant I was physically challenging my mind. It was one way I could ground myself. With all the transitions in my life, I found myself emotionally and spiritually centered through physical activity. I found my way of calming my anxiety and alleviating my depression.

CHAPTER 6

TAKE A DEEP BREATH

All I heard was a voice. I had no idea who had grabbed my hand, yet I squeezed it to let them know that I heard them. I was unaware that a mask covered my eyes. I tried opening them although could not see anything and went back to sleep.

Four days on a respirator, and finally the doctors removed the tube they had stuck down my throat. I remember taking a deep breath, which felt like I was gasping for air.

I was told that people who have been kept alive by a respirator for a long period of time sometimes develop complications, such as their body organs failing to function properly. With me, there was no kidney damage or organ damage. Simply, the lower left lobe of my lung was shattered from the bullet and thus was removed. I can live without part of my lung.

I asked to look in mirror once the tube came out and I was more conscious. I had been sleeping and on pain medication so I did not really know what was happening. I had not bathed for days. I imagine the nurses wiped my body down to some extent, yet tubes were still protruding from my sides and other places. Let's just say, I wouldn't be getting up to use the bathroom.

Someone handed me a small mirror. My hair was long and crusted with blood from when they found me laying down in the pew in the church.

Five days had gone by.

My face and neck were swollen and bruised. I asked someone why my face was black and blue. I was told that the swelling had gone down a great deal. Really? My neck had been swollen out to my face so it did not look like I had a neckline. The bruising was from losing so much blood and having it build up in my lungs and body before I was hustled out of the church and raced to the emergency room.

I can only imagine what I looked like to everyone in the intensive care unit.

A short time after the respirator had been removed, I remember the nurses and doctors coming back in to take me away. Because of all the pain medications I was given, I don't recall exactly what was happening. I do remember some people from school or family members were in my room, and as they were wheeling me back to surgery, I looked at them and told them not to worry, that I'd be right back. I had no idea that complications or internal bleeding started again, which was life threatening. I needed surgery immediately.

Thirty-six units of blood, two major surgeries, fragments of a bullet in my body, fighting for life in the intensive care, and hooked up to a respirator for four days.

But within a week, I was up and walking. I was slightly tilted when I walked at first because of my surgeries and the pain it caused. After about a week and a half, I was sent to the psychiatric ward a block away. I was transported by ambulance one block away even though I was more than willing to walk the one block.

Fear is a powerful force. People were fearful of me trying to run.

I was locked up for over a month. My clothes were too big since I lost weight in the hospital. I was not allowed a belt or string to hold my pants up, so I walked around holding them up with my hand.

I was sitting in my room at the psych ward and thinking about having no shoes, no belt, and what was going to happen from here.

CHAPTER 7
MY WORDS SPOKEN

It felt like people were staring at me. Slowly, I took my first steps outside my room in the psychiatric ward. My jeans were crunched up on the side in my hand, holding them up since I didn't have a belt. When they checked me into my room, my shoes were taken away, and they went through all my belongings. I was not allowed anything that I could use to harm myself.

I started to walk down the hall, tilting onto my left side because I was unable to stand up straight because of my surgery. I walked over and sat in a chair by the staff office, which was behind glass windows. I sat there feeling like everyone was staring at me although I did not know anyone. I remember looking around and thinking to myself, where am I.

During my time in the psychiatric ward, I sat in a group where I worked on my homework, so I would not fall behind in my classes or be held back a grade in high school. I was required to attend a group, yet I shared the bare minimum with everyone else in that space. Why would I share the details of my life? I was taught not to trust people, so what made people think I would open up now.

I went to a therapist a few times who was on another floor in the building although I did not share the depths of my life with her. I remember being angry about having to see the therapist. I shared very little about my life. The sense of rage buried within me--I didn't want anyone to see it.

When my mom would show her rage, people assumed she was crazy. I was determined not to be like my mom.

I connected with a few people over the course of my time living in a psychiatric unit. After being there about a week, one of the staff members sat next to me when I was sitting by the office and told me that when I smiled, my whole face changed. I looked at her and nodded my head. She said I should smile more often. Why would I smile more, I wondered. I was miserable.

With my stay coming to an end in the psych ward, my mom, aunt and uncle, and counselors at school were talking about where I would live and finish the school year. I remember very clearly someone telling me that the school did want me to return and that my aunt and uncle were hesitant to take me back into their home. My stomach sunk and my body filled with terror. What am I going to do? Where would I go to school? Where would I stay? I crumbled inside.

I assume my mom fought for me to return to the same high school and to stay with my aunt and uncle. However, the deal was that I had to attend therapy on a weekly basis and I was not allowed to use the word "fine." When my aunt asked me how I was doing, I would say, "I am fine." In reality, I hurt inside, badly. But there were no exceptions to the new rules I would have to live by. I agreed, even though I didn't want to go to therapy because I didn't believe it was helping me. Therapy only brought to the surface how angry I was with my life.

Finally, I was allowed to go back home, which was at my aunt and uncle's house. I was nervous to step back into their home. The last time I left was before shooting myself. I had left a note for them and my mom. I had placed all the clothes I wanted to be wearing when they buried me, along with instructions for my funeral on my bed. I knew the minister I wanted to give the service, the songs to be sung, and the prayers to be shared.

I was terrified and happy to be home. Happy to be out of a locked facility, yet unable to articulate all the emotions circulating within my body.

I went back to school the next day. Yet walking through the front doors and down the hall, I was overwhelmed with fear. Silence filled the hallway. I walked slowly to my locker. When passing people, I could feel them staring at me yet no words were being spoken. I felt like people just looked at me. They were stunned. Others had only heard about what happened at school on April 6, yet had not seen me in more than two months.

My teammates were the ones who made me feel the most comfortable. They welcomed me back into their everyday routines, and I sat on the bench with them until the season ended. No one asked questions. They made me feel not so alone.

A few days after returning to school, I had a therapy appointment to attend. I had a conversation with a close friend at school about how I was struggling and not happy. I also spoke with the school counselor beforehand who was concerned about my well-being. I was not smiling enough, which made some people worry that I'd try to kill myself again. When I went to my therapist's office on a lower level of the psychiatric ward, I thought I would get locked up again. I wouldn't be going home, I thought. That is exactly what happened.

People were terrified. People were nervous, watching me struggle day after day. I did not want to die. Yet, I had no idea how to live in the world. Even though I had lived away from my mother from the age of 15, I felt lost, had no social skills, and no idea what the future held for me. I was struggling to figure out my next steps, and all the people around me were focused on whether I would attempt suicide again. They were not focused on me. They were focused on their fear.

Watching someone in pain is incredibly difficult. Engaging with someone who is not meeting what society expects of someone at the age of 18 was a challenge. I didn't want to talk about the weather casually, what TV shows everybody was watching, or my plans to attend college after graduation. I was not meeting the socially acceptable norms, and it was difficult for some people to be with me. I had not lived a life of being raised by two parents, living in a stable home, being able to call friends and have them over for the night. I was raised in an underground and isolated way because of being homeless and poor. And I was unable to share this experience with anyone.

Growing up, I did not learn how to socially interact with friends. I did not relate to having the latest fashionable clothes or knowing the newest television sitcom. I did not have the luxury of a phone or television. In my senior year of high school, I had very little social skills and felt behind my peers in many ways.

I knew how to live and be with pain, anger, grief, and quietness. What I craved was someone to help me figure out how to live in this world, how to survive with all my emotions, and use them for my benefit. I had no idea how to interact with people socially or to ask for help. I had no idea how to trust someone. I did not trust that people would follow through with what they said they would do. I was lost and trying to teach myself how to interact with people. I would observe and watch from a distance how people interacted with one another.

Many years had passed before I really understood how to develop friendships. In all honesty,

I do not have many close friends now and really have only acquaintances in my life.

My former coach once told me I would only have only a handful of people in my life who I could rely on.

CHAPTER 8
WHO WOULD LISTEN

You never know what life has in store for you. Life has a way of unfolding before your eyes. I didn't understand this when I was younger. I was in pure survival mode. Day by day was all I could handle.

I would catch a glimpse occasionally of what I hoped my life would entail. I had dreams of owning a home, raising children, and traveling, dreams many people had. At times, I would think about running away, disappearing from anyone who knew me. I would reinvent myself.

California seemed like a great place to move to. I did not know anyone there. I could figure out how to work there.

The question is would I be starting a new life or running away from my history, legacy, my truth.

I also thought about becoming a hermit and living in the mountains. I would live in a log cabin, surrounded by wilderness, a lake close by, all by myself. No one to bother me. No one to hurt me. No more disappointment. I would live alone and work.

Fleeing to California or living in the mountains

became my dreams. My desire became to run away or hide from societies expectations. I would vision sitting on a porch in the woods, having coffee in the morning and a beer at night. Neither of these dreams became true.

Remember the conversation I had with my high school basketball coach, the phrase "believe in yourself, and you will succeed" stuck in my mind. My dreams were interrupted and put to rest after meeting with him. College became a possibility after our meeting. From there, I was on my path to discovering what life entails.

I still had dreams of getting married, owning a home, and raising children. I would enjoy being a parent. I knew I did not want to bring children into this world until I was in a position to financially support them. I did not want my children to experience what I went through when I was younger. I was committed to this vow. No child should have to face the pain, feelings of hopelessness, and struggles that my mom and I went through. As a possible parent, this was my commitment to my future children.

Also, I am an only child so I would not be an

uncle to any children. Yet, I will always be a supportive adult and champion for any young people in my life.

The reality is that too many children and young people are struggling. The sad part is that people are not willing to simply sit with the hurt and pain of a young person. The tendency is to try to fix the situation without really hearing where the pain is coming from.

I did not talk to anyone about my experiences with suicide and recovery and living in a car and being hungry and feeling deeply alone in this world. Who would listen? Who wanted to listen to me whine about my daily struggles? If I couldn't figure out how to navigate through this culture, how could anyone possibly help me?

Today, as I look back, I can honestly say that I don't regret my adolescence. Now, I know I can survive any situation presented to me. I have skills that many people have not tapped into within themselves. I am resilient, can live with pain, face hardships, and survive. I am willing to work anywhere if I need to make money. My mom said to me, "You know what it takes to do what you need to do in order to get through tough moments in life. Not everyone knows how to do that. You are a hard worker who cares about people."

Even when I'm financially strapped, I have learned how to stretch a dollar until my next paycheck. I will find work in a restaurant, retail store, or doing shipping and receiving labor in order to pay rent, eat, or put gas in my car. Do I want to work at retail positions or be in the service industry? It is not ideal, yet I will work.

I want to be at a point in my life where I am more financially secure. And I am on my way there even though it is later in my life. I cannot turn back and try to change decisions and actions from the past. I've taken responsibility for my insecurities and feelings of trying to live an unrealistic lifestyle. I learned this from my mother growing up as well as what other people, society, told me about how to live.

My mom wanted me to have the best in life. She wanted me to feel proud and have a warm and loving home where I could rest my head when needed.

Finally, I found my path in life. I invested in myself in so many ways. I focused on figuring out who I was, the way I wanted to be in the world, and how to truly live an authentic life. It is not easy. I have faith and trust in who I am and the ways I share myself and life daily with people.

I think of all the people who have money or present an image of a life full of material items, yet they have huge debt and don't feel fulfilled as a person. I tried to be somebody I wasn't. I tried to amass all the material stuff that I thought would show I belonged in society.

I belong. Today. Finally.

CHAPTER 9
DOING THE INTERNAL WORK

Life happens. We have a plan about what we want to accomplish throughout our lifetime; where we want to travel; a vision of our home, family relations, and all the other pieces of life that pop up.

Over the course of my lifetime, I have learned that life presents situations that may be challenging yet that I am able to handle. I use to get frazzled immediately. I was taught very few skills for dealing with stressful situations. I would ask, "Why is this happening to me" or "What did I do to deserve this." I would say to myself, "I can't take anymore" and would be overwhelmed by hopelessness.

At times, I felt immobilized to even think about solutions and taking actions to deal with the situation. For instance, I went home from school one day only to see an eviction notice on the door. I had no idea what that meant at the time. I went to unlock the door, and my key wouldn't work. I broke down in tears. Cell phones didn't exist in those days, so there I was, stuck outside our apartment, no way to call my mom, my kitten was inside, and I just stood there. Unable to move. Unable to think about what to do.

So, I walked to the library and used a phone there to call my mom. I told her I was locked out. Back on the streets we went.

Later in my life, these feelings still arise. My car broke down on my way home from work one day as I pulled off the interstate. All of a sudden, the engine quit at the stop sign. I tried to start it, and nothing would happen. "Are you serious?" I thought to myself. Holding back tears and frustration, I called a tow truck. All I kept thinking, "How will I pay for the tow and repairs for my car." I just couldn't catch a break. And I circled back to why this was happening to me. Turns out that it was the serpentine belt that needed to be replaced, so it was not as awful as it could have been.

I have learned to slow down when unexpected situations arise. I have moments of panic, especially when money is involved. Yet, I inherently know that no matter what the circumstances are--paying rent, making a car payment, towing a vehicle, changing jobs--that I can handle it. I have coped with many crises and near crises over the years, and I know when to keep my focus, stay calm, and take the necessary steps to move forward and that the fear about money, finding a job, or moving will work out. No matter the situation I encounter, I will survive. As long as I don't crack and fall into the emotional cracks that I did when I was younger, I won't lose it. No longer do I wilt into a puddle and fret over "What did I do to deserve this?"

There was a time when I gave myself a pity party about life and played the role of the victim-- instead of acknowledging that I had the mental fortitude to do what was needed to handle different situations. For instance, I know I have to pick up the phone to call the tow truck, show up for an interview even if I may not get the job, or ask for help financially. Growing up, I was alone, and my mom was asking for help from people all the time. Mainly, she asked if we could stay at their house. At some point, we stopped staying at people's home. For me, I was determined to not rely on someone else to help me out when unexpected and challenging situations would pop up.

If I moved from one apartment to the next, I moved myself. When I was in graduate school in California, I borrowed a dolly from the thrift store, loaded up a small couch, and walked a half mile down the street to my studio. I had the mentality that I could do it by myself because I had been for years.

Even today, I resist asking for help. I learned throughout the course of my life that I couldn't trust anyone, so why would I start later in my life. When you ask for help, you have to rely on someone else to follow through for you. Why would I expose myself to the potential hurt or disappointment? No thank you!

The reality is I have needed help in my life, and I do not want to live in isolation. At times, being alone sounded good, yet I really love being connected to someone and want to share my life with another person and have friends. My dreams have shifted slightly: I envision having a home, traveling, laughing, and enjoying adventures. Never before did those thoughts cross my mind.

I pay attention to my expectations of people and the people I am surrounded by. If I have unrealistic expectations of someone, I realize I might end up disappointed. I don't spend time with people who have unhealthy behaviors, such as spending a lot of time in bars or gossiping.

Life is valuable and very short. This is a new

way of thinking for me that I have worked to embrace. I looked at my past behaviors, the people I surrounded myself with, the societal expectations of who I am supposed to be, and decided to live my life differently. I decided to figure out how to navigate society and not let people's judgments of me impact how I live.

Every day, I practice following my dreams, staying true to myself, and doing my internal work, given the trauma I live with daily. Every day is a day of healing.

CHAPTER 10
STAYING CONNECTED

Too many people struggle with a sense of hopelessness about their lives--from my perspective. People feel a lack of connection, alone, and feel in subtle ways like they are isolated. Being an extreme introvert, I can state unequivocally that I am not unfamiliar with time spent alone. My behavioral patterns have become ingrained over the years of being by myself and doing things on my own. Do I prefer to be connected to people? Yes, I enjoy having a relationship, although I am not inclined to have a large social group of friends. My level of trust with people is minimal, and I struggle to engage in small talk or gossip on a regular basis.

At times, feelings of hopelessness seep in, and I ask myself just what it is that I am really doing in my life. Yet, I know the feelings will pass as long as I keep my focus. For me, staying connected to people is secondary to staying connected with who I am as a person. What are my values, beliefs, and what people do I want to be surrounded with in my life? Now in my life, I do not lose sight of this aspect. I lean on my values and beliefs to get me through difficulties or times when I question my life.

Over the years, I don't feel like I've openly shared what I've encountered in my life with my family or individuals I try to connect with on a more intimate level. Often, I do not believe that details of my life are important to share. However, I've made it through rough days, months and years, not necessarily smoothly and not without a lot of internal homework.

I have spent many months in therapy, have engaged with others in peer groups, and have talked to people about my struggles. I had to take a look at the ways I would try to fit in to groups of people, such as showing up at happy hours, buying a Jeep Wrangler to go four-wheeling with the guys, getting a motorcycle, and attending conferences on an annual basis even though I could not afford it. Actually, I ended up financially struggling trying to connect to people through material items instead of by building relationships on emotional and spiritual levels.

Silence about the feelings of hopelessness manifest over time until it may be too late. Until someone decides to give up trying to emotionally connect with others, they cope with the pain through alcohol, drugs, buying things they don't need, excessive eating, and taking part in other coping mechanisms, just to get through the day. Others may attempt or commit suicide. The feelings of hopelessness can be overwhelming.

As I was mired in those feelings and barely survived my suicide attempt, I had my fair share of trying to numb or run away from my feelings of despair, isolation, or disappointment. Hurt. Pain. Loneliness.

What was I running from? I was running from myself, who I was in this world, the gifts I have to offer people. I am not a novice by any means with knowing how to navigate life. I am willing to show up day after day to face what life offers me. Fear of deeply connecting with myself holds the power and success of my life.

Holding a gun to my heart and pulling the trigger can create a shock effect to many people. I have learned how to deal with this shock on some level because of having to explain to doctors over and over why I have needed lung surgery. You know, the common questions we are asked at the doctor's office.

Next time you go, pay attention to the question about having had surgeries. What is your response?

Over many decades, I never fully addressed the underlying emotions that led me to feeling that death was the only way out. I never talked about being homeless as an adolescent; moving away from my mother at age 15; feeling alone in my life; and figuring out how to survive in this world, given all the cultural expectations put on us.

I should be financially stable, have children, and be debt-free by the time I am 40. But that has not been my story. It has not been my path.

In my 20s, I was trying to fit in to groups of people so that I might have close friends. I worked at a nightclub because it was where I could get a job and made a lot of money. I graduated late from undergraduate school so I never had the four-year experience or developed friendships during my college years.

I did not understand that I was emotionally and spiritually struggling to connect with people. I surrounded myself with acquaintances, not friends. I went to happy hours and realized later on that I was slowly killing myself by drinking too much alcohol and eventually trying cocaine with people where I worked. I made a lot of money as a general manager and bartender at a nightclub. I thought I had finally gained status in the world. I resisted doing any form of drugs for a long period of time until one night I decided to snort a line of cocaine. I was immediately hooked. I had found another way to escape from dealing with my emotions, my feelings of loneliness and hurt.

One Saturday night, we were busy earlier than normal, and I was the only one working. The other staff did not arrive until 10 p.m. because we did not get busy until late at night. Upon trying cocaine and getting hooked right away, I found myself working high at the nightclub in order to make it through the night. This one Saturday night, I did not have any drugs on me, was waiting for my staff to arrive, could not find anyone who had any drugs, and found myself angry, absolutely frustrated with my staff because I needed help.

A light clicked in my head: I was turning into someone else, not the person I was internally. I felt lost, and realized I had no friends, no connections with anyone. I was dying inside slowly because of feelings of hopelessness. Somehow, I wasn't measuring up to what society expected of me. I didn't know how to articulate what was happening at the time. Therapy and meeting others who faced similar struggles helped me understand that it was not my fault.

That is the piece to focus on: I needed help and could not figure out who I could rely on. I was alone once again in my life. Throughout that night, I realized I was out of control because of alcohol and cocaine. I thought to myself, "Someone is going to overdose soon," and I did not want to be that person. I was slowly committing suicide. Yet, I was tired of running away from my feelings. I wanted out of the business. After that night, I was done working in that environment and feeling like this was the only place to connect to people.

I was very secretive about using drugs and getting hooked so quickly. I used for about six months; my skin was turning yellow, and I looked sickly. I hid my using from people as best I could. I was ashamed of my behavior and was losing sight of myself. Yet I was in so much pain, and my solution at the time was to numb all my feelings.

We all have feelings. We have different and complex lived experiences. We have the opportunity to live a vibrant and abundant life. That's our decision. I decided to stop running from who I was as a person. To be myself, I became willing to lose any relationships I had. Internally, I accepted the fact that I might live the rest of my life alone. And I decided I could live with that.

After making this decision, my life found its way onto the path that was meant for me. I started working as a security officer at a university, which led me to apply for graduate school. I was willing to be cracked open emotionally and spiritually. I was willing-that's the key phrase here. My life would look different if I had not been willing or resisted change. I would still be struggling with those overwhelming feelings of hopelessness.

I have fumbled throughout the past many years, yet I always circle back to keeping myself open and willing to possibilities. It is a challenge when the pressure intensifies to try to fit into society's expectations, especially as I age. My life has brought me to where I am today. I show up everyday. I love deeply my partner, her children, our families, and understand that we have a level of connection beyond words.

Every day is a new day. Every day is a practice for me. A practice of believing in myself, trusting my vision of life, reflecting on my fears, and knowing I will figure out the steps needed to take so I can move forward. It might not be on society's timeline or in alignment with cultural expectations. I have learned to let go of those expectations and to stop burdening myself with them.

I have taken responsibility for my actions, not walked away from my insecurities but faced them, and sat with feelings of concern, fear, and worry. I also feel joy, love, supported, happiness, and excitement. I embrace all of my feelings and allow them to flow through my body, my bloodstream. I know I am not alone, even though it might seem like I am at times. I am never alone.

This book, my experience, is to let people know they are not alone and that one can survive in this world. One can survive and get through the feelings of hopelessness that might exist in their lives.

Someone might never know what the person in front of you has experienced. In many ways, I have been silent about my experiences. I realized that my story could assist someone so that they might feel connected and not isolated. If we can share openly the challenges and struggles of our trauma or lived experiences, who knows what can manifest or who we might connect with.

Shame does not have to be the driver in sharing our life. Hope can be the one in the driver's seat. Possibilities can be the passenger.

CHAPTER 11

FEELINGS OF COMFORT

Remember the days back when you were a kid and had that favorite stuffed animal? You would take that stuffed animal everywhere you went, and it gave you a sense of comfort when you needed it. Snoopy was the stuffed animal who gave me that sense of comfort.

Snoopy was my best pal when I was a kid. I would drag him around by the arms or the ears till they got worn out. His arms would be dangling there, and he would have half an ear left. Every year I would have to get a new Snoopy, and he meant just as much every year.

Snoopy had clothes for the different seasons. He had shorts, T-shirts, jeans with suspenders that I had made so he could keep his pants on, a jogging suit, tennis shoes, a leather jacket, and of course, pajamas.

When I was younger, I would get car sick when we drove a long distance. One time when we were coming home from my grandma's, I was sitting in the front seat with Snoopy and I lost it. I had vomited all over the front seat, myself, and Snoopy. My mom turned around because it was closer just to go back to my grandma's. She took Snoopy away and threw him, along with his clothes, in the washing machine. I felt so awful and all alone. After he was cleaned, my mom returned him to me. Then, I was comforted.

When I would get in trouble for doing something, I would grab my Snoopy and run into my room. If I was angry at my mom or something else, I'd take Snoopy by his dangling arms and smash his little stuffed body against the wall. Then I would punt him across the room or again against the wall. Afterwards, I felt so awful and would apologize my little heart out. Through all that, he was always my friend and always gave me that feeling that everything was going to be alright.

When I was in the hospital, my cousin sneaked Snoopy into the intensive care unit. Snoopy was zipped up in his jacket. When he unzipped his jacket and I saw Snoopy in there, I reached as hard as possible, but it was difficult in my condition. Snoopy understood. My cousin set him up by my head on my bed, and Snoopy remained there until I left. He gave me that sense of comfort and that feeling of everything would work out.

Snoopy has given me that sense of comfort whenever I needed it. It is funny how I turned to something so small like a stuffed animal to give me the feeling that everything will be all right.

Snoopy will be in my suitcase wherever I may end up. I'm sure, someday, I'll pass him on to a small person who needs that same comfort.

CHAPTER 12
WHO IS DRIVING?

Often times, doubt will enter my mind about the direction of my life and what I am meant to be doing in this world. Once in a while, I will get a glimpse and acknowledge the gifts I have to offer people. However, I find myself tired of struggling financially and bumping up against feelings of inadequacy. At moments of transition with employment, I think to myself "Is my financial situation ever going to get better," "Am I going to find a job that pays me a decent wage that I can live off comfortably and retire in the future," and "What are my steps to find a career that I love doing?" The answer is simple.

Keep walking my path, stay focused, and believe in myself. Keep my vision alive.

Not easy to do mentally. Especially when the reality of paying bills and the struggles of life unfold. I have learned and witnessed in my life that walking my path is a daily practice and challenging times in life will always emerge. Challenging moments are the ways I deepen my practice and belief in my capacity.

I continue to show up every day for life and do my best to be present with what the universe shows me. At times, I put one foot in front of the other, pause to take a deep breath, and keep moving forward. Deepening my awareness and practice to be compassionate and patient. My spiritual practices entails simply waking up, venturing for a run, and walk through the day physically and emotionally present the best I can that day. Doubt enters my mind although insecurity does not rule my spiritual tenacity. Fear exists yet is not going to overtake the driving in my life. It may be in the back seat trying to jump up front, however, a daily practice has provided me with mental and emotional tools to keep it at bay.

Life is challenging, beautiful, and constantly changing. I have learned how to move with the flow of my life, keep the circulation of giving and receiving active, do my best not to become stagnant in my thoughts, actions and practices. I lean into trusting the universes process with unfolding my vision and my purpose in life. It is not on my timeline, I do not have control. I would like to at times. However, I have found it does not work for me to try and be the director.

I can be the driver with hope and possibilities being the director, I put my foot on the pedal and stay on the path that is meant for me to follow. I have the option of veering off, and I have veered off in my life only to realize the direction I was headed really was not meant for me.

Lesson learned and notes taken not to venture down that road again.

Back on track and keeping my focus. Scared, excited, doubtful, and all the other emotions that emerge in walking through life. I feel those emotions today, I notice them, I listen to my inner self, and I trust in my faith that the universe is taking care of me, my family and people in my world.

Fear is not the driver today. It keeps trying to get a hold of the wheel. Hope and possibility are my companions. I sit with the suffering being experienced in our society. The pain, rage, and grief are felt. The review mirror allows me to witness what I have passed through in my life, so I can be fully present today. Fear may still be lingering in the back seat, which is welcomed to remind me that I am alive. Moving towards success and living a big life is scary.

As I glance back, I see all that I have walked through, driven by and survived in my life to bring to this point today.

Fear is not the driver, today.

CHAPTER 13

TRANSITIONS IN LIFE

Transitions in life are inevitable. They will happen at various points in one's lifetime. One of the gifts I have been given in my life is learning how to navigate transitions throughout my life. Being raised without a stable home has taught me a plethora of lessons that I can sit back and reflect on now. In the moment, at age 10, I felt my life was falling apart. And it was falling apart in my mind.

My life did not align with societies standards of having a two-parent household. My parents were in court going through a battle with one another to gain custody of me. I recall sitting in the Judge's chambers and him asking me whether I wanted to live with my mom or dad. Seriously, you are going to make me decide where I wanted to live? In the early 1980's, single family households were not as common as they are today. I told him that I wanted to live with my mom.

Little did I know at the age of 10 the depth of this decision. At many points in my life, I made decisions based on trying to fit into the expectations of society. I tried to fit in to what was deemed 'normal' or expected of me.

I have these thoughts of being more financially stable, a robust retirement fund, out of debt, and all the other aspects tied up with financial components of life. The financial aspects of life are what overwhelm me because of being raised poor, being homeless throughout my life, relying on other people to help us financially. I had to learn to be financially independent, yet had many people take advantage of my financial generosity.

Transitions in life are a challenge. Finally, I am done trying to "Keep up with the Jones." I may internally fumble around about not having a plethora of money. Yet, the reality is I have no idea what the status of peoples' finances who presume to have money. Do you they have large credit card bills? Did they receive an inheritance? How did their parents financially help them throughout their lives?

I realize life is much more than money or material items. We live in a society that appears to value the materialistic aspects of our lives. From my perspective, we build connections on the things we possess instead of the in-depth conversations about our histories or lived experiences.

Throughout my life, I have been faced with transitions and making decisions about my life. Knowing that I may be alone until my life comes to an end. I was constantly searching for someone to model my life after and realize there is no one. My life experiences are my model. My sense of self, who I am and what I believe are my foundation. In a world where persistent societal expectations of what I should be doing in my life or where I should be at with a career or finances, I pause and decide to do it differently. My reality is different than societal expectations. I refuse to become hooked into societies or other peoples' fear.

In the financial realm, money continues to flow in my life as long as I continue to be clear with the giving and receiving flow of funds. I do not fear money, yet I am not going to live out of my means again or pretend to be someone I am not. I do not fear life. Nor death.

Looking back on my life, I was given the gift of being fully present throughout all my struggles. I have been provided an opportunity to reflect on what my life entailed, feel the pain, the struggles, awakenings, and visions of where my life is going. I am emotionally and spiritually wealthy where many people are faced with distractions from tuning into their emotions or spiritual challenges.

I have been given the gift of transitions, making a decision to be who I am, and knowing how to be still and alone, yet I am never alone in this world. I trust in a process and stay emotionally and spiritually open to follow my path with all the bumps in the road, storms that emerge, and potential detours that are encouraged.

Life is a constant state of transition. For me, this is the beauty of life. Our bodies, minds and spirits are constantly changing, growing, aging, and it is my decision on how to be with all those changes.

I witnessed throughout my years what it means to play the victim of life circumstances. I refuse to embrace this mentality. My life may appear difficult to some people. I may get exhausted and desire a different path at times, however, I will continue to move forward with my life and do whatever it takes to survive. I have learned to survive – no matter what. My life matters.

Afterword

During the years I composed and wrote this book, I was asked from time to time to explain why I did not weave my struggle with gender identity into its chapters.

I have pondered that question. And yes, my identity as a transgender man indeed has been one of my nearly lifelong struggles. One of my explanations for that aspect of my life not being central to this book is that people tend to fixate on an individual being transgender and fail to recognize other valuable aspects of someone's life.

It was important to me that the fact that I am a transgender man not become the book's focal point. At some later moment in my life, I intend to describe and explain in another book my process of transitioning.

My life has been a complex mix of struggles and challenges and high points and low moments and distress and joy and triumph. I have walked in many shoes, not all of which fit comfortably. This book was about sharing a silent story, particularly my suicide attempt, and what led me to such a place of pain and hopelessness. It's a story that few people who knew me were aware of, and it was almost never talked about in my family when I was released from the hospital and mental health facility

Prior to publishing this book, I shared its content with my wife, mother, my aunt and uncle, as well as close, extended family members. It was important to me that I shared my story with only those people. I was living with my aunt and uncle at the particularly devastating moment when I pulled the trigger on a gun in an attempt to end my life. It was that gun that in a roundabout way saved my life. This book is a story I have carried with me throughout my life, and sharing it now with others is a healing process not only for me but for my family. I hope my story will interrupt the lingering decades of silence of pain and hurt that have lived in our hearts and bodies.

When I was 30 years old, I made a very clear decision to begin transitioning and to accept what being transgender would mean for me. I was aware that that decision might include the possibility of being alone for the rest of my life. I accepted that. I had dreamed of someday having a partner and nurturing a family and of possibly being a daddy. I was fully aware that that life-changing decision might preclude all of that. Today, I have a deeply loving and supportive wife and family who accept me for who I am as a transgender person and all my lived experiences. I am incredibly grateful for who she is and her ways of walking through this world. I share with her, our family, and all the young people in our orbit, the notion of endless possibilities that our life together and individually today have to offer, even when times may be a struggle.

For me, this book was a catharsis. It allowed me to break the near silence of my life's story. Even though the details of my struggles certainly are not identical to the struggles of other people, I hope my story of survival can bring hope to others. It is my hope that those who read the story of how I struggled with hopelessness can also emerge from such darkness with an energy of hope and a belief that anything is possible.

By reading this book, I hope other people will find the strength to openly share their lived realities and will engage in a healing process beyond what today might be difficult to comprehend. For me, this book was a healing process, and it is my hope that it also will be a healing process for my family, my extended family, and for generations to come.

ABOUT THE AUTHOR

Jordon Johnson Chisti, PhD, holds a doctoral degree in American Studies from the University of New Mexico. He is the Executive Director of Life House, an organization in Duluth, Minnesota, that works with homeless and struggling youth between the ages of 14 and 24.

This book, his first, describes how he embraces his deep spiritual practice and faith in the universe. It also shares a story about a life journey in which he plunged to depressing lows and climbed up and through challenging moments to experience a life of accomplishments and successes. He strives to share with people who have struggled with feelings of hopelessness and identity issues that anything in life is possible.

He believes in being attentive and listening to the messages shared throughout his days as a guide and trusts a process that may not be fully known to him. Jordon lives in Duluth with his wife, Kristy Marie, and their family.

Made in the USA
Monee, IL
09 July 2022

99329852R00046